THE GREEN BOOK
OF THE

Melissa Kelley

THE GREEN BOOK
OF THE

Santa Muerte

Melissa Kelley

Introduction

Today, the cult of Santa Muerte has gradually spread to different regions of Latin America. In some places it is called "San Muerte" in Argentina for example and in Mexico La Santa Muerte, La Santísima or "La Niña Blanca" It is in Mexico where the cult of death is a little more versatile, broad and inclusive with some peculiarities that make it simply unique. And it is that believers aware of the threats of their own environment, such as violence, insecurity, disinterest on the part of the authorities and uncertainty in their own lives.

seek refuge in a cult that somehow provides them with hope or security in the present, which otherwise they would never be able to obtain. And the truth is that for a long time it was believed that only those who live in constant danger profess such belief, for example: policemen, drug traffickers, prostitutes, criminals, etc. But the cult is transversal to different social groups and socioeconomic levels, those who used to hide such belief now show it publicly.

Within the cult to the Santísima Muerte there is a variant in the colors of the attire that represent the Santa Muerte, such variant is due to the fact that each color is used with different purposes within the rituals of the cult, for example: The white color "protection", the red color "Love" etc. In this case we will focus on the Santa Muerte green color whose meaning represents within the cult "Justice" this image of the Santísima is very used by lawyers, judges, criminals and policemen. Her direct influence acts on any situation of legal nature, injustices, problems with contracts, imprisonment, etc.

Dear reader, in this book you will find spells, invocations and prayers, through which you will be able to work directly with the power of the green Santa Muerte, change the course of your legal problems at will, get rid of what hinders you and learn to manipulate the universal law in your favor through the unique power of Santa Muerte that without prejudice is there to help you in any obstacle you have, no matter how difficult it may seem.

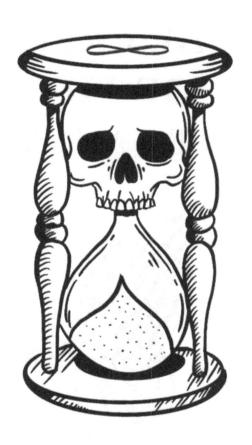

THE CREED
OF THE
SANTA MUERTE

I believe in you, Most Holy Death,
righteous, powerful and omnipotent
lady,
faithful handmaid of God the Father,
that in your hands we shall
to the reunion of our Lord God.
Lord God.

I believe in you, Most Holy Death, that
with your scythe you remove all
obstacles
from our path and cut off all evil
I believe in you Most Holy Death, that
with your divine balanced scales
justice will be in my favor and with your
powerful gaze you protect me from all
danger.
from all danger.

I believe in you, faithful servant of God,
Most Holy Death, and I will always
believe,
for here I sign with my hand so that you
may know that I will never cease to
believe in you.

What a pact with you Santa Muerte, so
that in exchange for my faith and eternal
love
you will always protect me.

I believe in you Most Holy Death for the
divine grace of God and I reject every evil
power.
I reject every evil power that can take
possession of my will, because
everything that you have to grant me
today and always has to be exclusively
with the permission of God the Father.

I believe in you, Most Holy Death, with love I say it, because I have placed my sorrows and sadness in you
I have deposited my sorrows and sadness in you and because every time I invoke your help and your name, you do it promptly and effectively.

I believe in you, Most Holy Death, because in this way I am protected against wind and tide.
I am blessed and there is no one who can harm me.

I worship and adore you my faithful guardian.
Most Holy Death, I quote my creed
I give to you

the promise never to decline in my faith,
of what it is to be a good child of God.
until the day he calls me.
so be it and so it shall be.

Amen.

PRISONER'S PRAYER

Oh my most Holy Death!

I (your name) ask you for my speedy release from this dreary place.

For the speeding up of my legal situation
since I cannot bear to be in this place one more minute, I ask you with all my heart to free me from all the obstacles placed by my enemies, both visible and invisible.

My Blessed Mother, I implore your constant help to be able to survive in this place.

this horrible place in which I am imprisoned today because of my clumsiness and all the mistakes I have made in my life, help me to have peace of mind to be able to overcome this sorrow that overwhelms me today.

Most Holy Death, I (your name) bow at your feet and take refuge in your lap so that you may protect me from any danger that assaults me in this place, thank you my White Child for the help that you give me daily.

Amen.

Note: This prayer should be done every day at 11pm for four weeks, at the time the prayer is being done, your family members should light a green candle and place it on the altar of the green Santa Muerte, if they do not have an altar, they can place the candle at the foot of a figure of the Blessed Mother or next to an image of the green Santa Muerte.

PROTECTION
PRAYER

You know well beloved death that danger and adventure are part of the road I travel in this life.

Allow beloved death that your protection and safeguard be always by my side, to keep me distant from any danger and threat.

Allow beloved death that the eyes of my opponents see neither my presence
nor the traces of my footsteps
that lead to your sacred temple, where majestic you patiently await until the end of my time.

Amen.

PRAYER
FOR
DIFFICULT
CASES

Before you I come my most holy death with the faith of my soul to seek your sacred consolation in this difficult situation; I ask you not to forsake me white lady, and that the doors that are to be opened in my path; be thanks to your powerful scythe to give me the tranquility that I so much longed for in these moments.

Today I come to you with an afflicted heart so that you help me with this supplication (make the petition) my white girl I ask you to please intercede for me in this so overwhelming occasion, since I would not want to succumb for the lack of your help.

Mighty Santa Muerte assist me, protect me, protect me and grant me what I ask of you, thank you for listening to my supplications, so be it.

Amen.

PRAYER
TO WIN
IN A TRIAL

Blessed Santa Muerte!

Protector of the weak and of justice.

You who look into the heart of the bad
and the good.

To you, my lady, I come to implore
justice, I ask for the impartiality of your
scales.

My Lady... see into my heart
hear my pleas that come out of
necessity.

Let your justice be done on earth, let your divine hand guide the decisions of judges and jailers.

Great lady... be implacable with the wicked
the wicked who reoffend, just with the innocent and benevolent with those who repent in heart and spirit.

Oh White Child!

Hear my prayers and protect me from inequity and indolence.

This day I ask your favor, that my case may be submitted to your measure and obtain the absolute pardon of the earthly judges.

In due time you will judge me and take the words I now pledge as the measure of my punishment or my acquittal.

Amen.

SPELL
TO HELP A
PRISONER

MATERIALS

A green candle.

An image of Santa Muerte in green.

A piece of wood found in the street.

OPERATION

On a Thursday at 11pm in a solitary place in your home and without any witness you should light the candle and place it at the feet of the image of the Most Holy Death, then recite the following prayer with a lot of faith, in one part of the prayer it says the following:

"My Lady, see that I ask you as I break this wood, that the grill that imprisons (name of the person)
be broken and set him free".

Just at that moment take the piece of wood and break it with all your strength in half, mentally visualizing how the bars of the cell that imprison your loved one are broken.

At the end of the prayer you must let the candle burn so that your petition flows through it, when the candle is completely consumed, keep the remnants of the candle and the image in a safe place.

This spell is very powerful and you only need to cast it once, following the steps to the letter, you will get the results in a very short time.

CONJURE

In the name of the Most Holy Death!

Mistress and mistress of the night, who sees and hears everything...

I (your name) break one of the bars that binds you...

(say the name of the person imprisoned)

My hands are not mine, they belong to the one who can do all things and to whom I entrust you.

My Lady, behold, I ask you as I break
this wood, that the grill that imprisons
(name the person) may break and set
him free, that there may be no power
on earth to keep him prisoner.
may it break and set him free, that
there be no power on earth to keep him
prisoner.

Oh Holy Death, omnipotent Mistress
I earnestly ask you to grant my plea....

(mention the full name of the person
imprisoned)

He promises you...

(mention the inmate's promise)
In exchange for his freedom.

In the name of the Almighty, may your
will always be done!

Amen.

PROTECTION
PRAYER

Santa Muerte dearest of my heart, do not forsake me of your protection.
I ask you to cover my home, work or business from this moment on.

So that you attract the positive energies of the universe and that nothing is ever lacking.
that all my needs be covered by the divine energy of God my father.
of God the Father.

By the virtues that you possess I will be able to overcome all obstacles and people who wish me harm will not get in my way, but positive people who only know how to love and respect humans who inhabit this planet.

I do not aspire for riches, but for a just life without lack of anything. protect me by day and by night.
so be it and so shall it be.

Amen.

PRISONER'S
PRAYER

Dear and Benevolent Most Holy Death!

Today at this hour, I prostrate myself before your altar to ask your forgiveness for the mistakes committed in my past; I ask you with all my heart to help me find the path that will lead me to the forgiveness of the Almighty, of you and of all those who judge me, help me to walk the middle path, the one that is right there, between good and evil, since I know that my behavior is not exactly the right one, but I would like to be a different person and I know that I will get it, thanks to your infinite goodness.

Today that I am in these bars that imprison me, give me the necessary strength to be able to fly to freedom.

Open with your infinite power the hearts of the people and the society that judges me, take care of me and protect me from my enemies today and always have mercy and free me
as soon as possible from this dark place.
dark place.

When I look at your face I realize that I belong to you and I will go hand in hand with you until the day of my final judgment, in the meantime I ask and beg you to intercede for me today.

My Dear Little White Girl, before the Creator, on this day and at this hour I thank you My Dear Little Fairy.

Amen.

PRAYER
TO WIN
IN A TRIAL

Oh Most Holy Death!

You know my heart and the truth behind all this unnecessary lawsuit.

I ask that in this difficult moment of my life you support me and give me the strength to face this legal problem that not only affects me, but also my loved ones.

I am a victim of this accusation and I want the truth to come out and only you my beautiful girl are the only one who can help me.

You know the truth and who are the people who are only trying to hurt me, because you are the advocate of good and you will intercede for me before GOD the Father.

By means of this little prayer I beg you to intercede for me before GOD so that divine justice may be present in this trial.

Do not allow the hearts of the judges, prosecutors and lawyers to be corrupted, and lead them on the path of justice.

Amen!

PROTECTION
AGAINST
ENEMIES

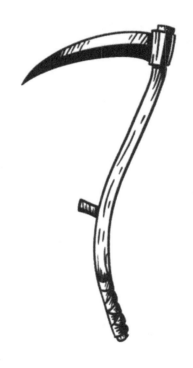

Oh Most Holy Death!

Today on this day I ask you to protect me
from all my enemies....

if they have eyes, let them not see me
if they have hands, let them not touch
me
if they have feet, let them not reach me
do not allow them to surprise me from
behind and do not allow my blood to be
shed, do not allow my blood to be spilled
let not my blood be shed, let not my
death be violent, let not envy destroy me,
let me not starve, let me not live in
disgrace, let not my ways be closed, let
not wickedness destroy me, and let not
my

enemies see me fall, you who know
everything, you know my sins as well as
my great faith, never forsake me,
my Most Holy Death.

Amen.

SPELL
TO LEAVE
FROM JAIL

MATERIALS

A black Santa Muerte candle

A large piece of rattlesnake skin

A black marker

A piece of white paper

A photo of the inmate

An insole of a shoe worn by the
person in confinement

Note: This spell is for people who are already incarcerated inside a prison or who are in danger of entering, no matter if they are guilty or not, in fact if they are guilty it works even better.

OPERATION

This spell should be performed on a Saturday at 11pm, the first thing to do is to take the insole of the shoe and with the help of the marker draw the shape of it on the skin of the snake in this way:

FIG. 01

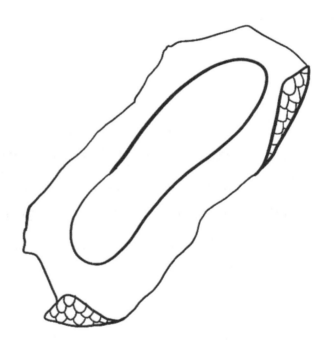

Once the template has been marked on the skin, the figure should be cut out with scissors, so that only the figure of the foot remains on the snakeskin.

The next step will be, with the same marker write the full name of the person and the date of birth, on the skin already cut out.

EXAMPLE

Francisco Tejeda
07-05-1987

Once this is done, take the piece of paper and write on it the full names of the people who are accusing you or are against you, including the plaintiff, police, lawyers and judges if possible, all the people who want you to be locked up.

At the end you will arrange everything in this order: first the template cut out on the skin of the snake (with the name written upwards) on top of this the piece of paper with the names of those who accuse you, above the names put the photograph of the prisoner.

(with the image upwards) on top of the photograph the template used by the person, with which at the beginning you marked the piece of skin and finally, on top of everything described above, place the black candle of the Most Holy Death.

*Before lighting the candle, with the black marker write on the glass the full name of the prisoner (it doesn't matter if you can't see it).

Everything should look like this:

Once everything is in the indicated order, light the candle, it is very important that you know that once lit and before it is completely consumed, you must light another one and so on until the person is released from prison, it is usually in a very short period of time, in rare cases it takes longer than expected.

This is a very powerful spell, if you have followed the indications to the letter and without omitting any step.

This is a very powerful spell, if you have followed the indications to the letter and without omitting any step, be sure that it will work without any doubt. be sure that without any doubt it will work.

Lastly, you should know that when you leave or do not enter prison, when the person arrives home, you should immediately thank immediately to Santa Muerte in case you have made a pact or a promise with the Blessed Virgin, when you are free you must respond and comply with what you have promised, because in case of not to do so, things can change from one moment to the next and this time the situation in which the person would find himself would be worse.

PRAYER
OF GRATITUDE

Thank you, Most Holy Death dear!

I (your name) thank you today for all the doors that you have opened for me, but even more strongly I thank you for all the doors that you closed, so that I could protect myself from all my enemies!

Amen.

PRAYER
FOR
WIN
IN A TRIAL

My beautiful child, I ask you to advocate for me, since only you know what my heart and soul feel, as well as all that I carry on my back.

You know that many times, I have done good without any interest.

But you also know that it is not always possible to keep everyone happy.

I ask you to protect me from all the infamies that come out of their mouths, I pray for your help my White Child.

Today on this day, I (say your name) come to seek you as my advocate and my savior, from the bottom of my heart I humbly beg you to help me in this difficult case.

(say the petition)

For you know very well that everything my accusers say is unjust and a total lie.

My Most Holy Death, come to my aid!

For I need you as my advocate to help me win in this trial so that injustice will not be done to me.

Amen.

The right hand of Santa Muerte has shown its strength; the right hand of Santa Muerte has shown its power, taking me out of this confinement.

The right hand of Santa Muerte has given proof of its infinite grace.

I will regain my freedom and I will be able to sing the marvels of the Most Holy Death, and to address my praises to him, may it be so.

Amen.

Dear readers, we have reached the end of this book, I recommend you to follow the instructions of each ritual to the letter and to have a strong conviction and unbreakable will in order to obtain the desired success in any magical work.

THE END

Document Outline

-
-